CONTENTS

DIAGONAL RIB Blanket

MEASUREMENTS
Approx 36 x 38" [91.5 x 96.5cm].

GAUGE
16 sts and 19 rows = 4" [10cm] with
2 strands tog in stockinette stitch.
Take time to check your gauge.

INSTRUCTIONS
Note Entire blanket is worked holding
2 strands of yarn tog.
Cast on 166 sts. Do not join in rnd.
Working back and forth across needle,
proceed as follows:
1st row (WS) K4. *(P2. K2) 5 times.** K3.
(K2. P2) 5 times. K3. Rep from * twice more,
then from * to ** once. K4.

2nd and alt rows K4. Knit all knit sts and purl
all purl sts as they appear to last 4 sts. K4.
3rd row K4. *P2tog. (K2. P2) 4 times. K2.
M1P.** K3. M1P. (K2. P2) 4 times. K2. P2tog.
K3. Rep from * twice more, then from * to
** once. K4.
5th row K4. *K2tog. K1. (P2. K2) 4 times. P1.
M1.** K3. M1. P1. (K2. P2) 4 times. K1. K2tog.
K3. Rep from * twice more, then from * to
** once. K4.
7th row K4. *K2tog. (P2. K2) 4 times. P2.
M1.** K3. M1. P2. (K2. P2) 4 times. K2tog.
K3. Rep from * twice more, then from * to
** once. K4.
9th row K4. *P2tog. P1. (K2. P2) 4 times. K1.
M1.** K3. M1. K1. (P2. K2) 4 times. P1. P2tog.
K3. Rep from * twice more, then from * to
** once. K4.
10th row As 2nd row.

Rep 3rd to 10th rows until Blanket measures 38" [96.5cm], ending with a WS row.
Cast off in Pat.

SPRING Square Blanket

YOU'LL NEED

YARN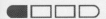
Bernat® Baby Coordinates (5oz/140g)
Contrast A 2 balls
(48615 Lemon Custard)
Contrast B 2 balls (48320 Soft Mauve)
Contrast C 2 balls (48228 Iced Mint)
Contrast D 1 ball (48738 Soft Turquoise)

NEEDLES
Size 9 (5.5mm) knitting needles
or size to obtain gauge

MEASUREMENTS
Approx 36" [91.5cm] square.

GAUGE
15 sts and 30 rows = 4" [10cm] with 2 strands tog in garter stitch.
Take time to check your gauge.

INSTRUCTIONS
Note Entire blanket is worked holding 2 strands of yarn tog.

Block A (make 9)
With A, cast on 23 sts.
Work in garter stitch (knit every row) until work from beg measures 6" [15cm].
Cast off.

Block B (make 9)
Work as for Block 1, substituting B for A.

Block C (make 9)
Work as for Block 1, substituting C for A.

Block D (make 9)
Work as for Block 1, substituting D for A.

FINISHING
Sew blocks tog, following Diagram. Have ridges running horizontally on every other block and vertically on alternate blocks.

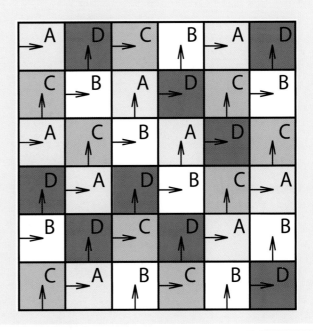

GARTER Stitch Blanket

YOU'LL NEED

YARN ③
Bernat® Baby Coordinates (5oz/140g)
1 ball each
Main Color (MC) (48615 Custard)
Contrast A (48228 Mint)
Contrast B (48005 White)

NEEDLES
Size 6 (4mm) knitting needles. Size
6 (4mm) circular knitting needle 24"
[60cm] long *or size to obtain gauge*

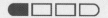

MEASUREMENT
Approx 30 x 35" [76 x 89cm].

GAUGE
22 sts and 30 rows = 4" [10cm] with larger
needles in stockinette st.
Take time to check your gauge.

INSTRUCTIONS
Strip I (make 3)
With B, cast on 27 sts.
1st row (WS) Knit.
**2nd and 3rd rows With A, knit.
4th and 5th rows With B, knit.
Rep last 4 rows of Stripe Pat until work
from beg measures 5" [12.5cm], ending
with 2 rows of A.
With B, work 5" [12.5cm] in stockinette st,
ending with a purl row.**
Work from ** to ** substituting MC for A.
Work from ** to ** as given above. Cast off.

Strip II (make 2)
With B, cast on 27 sts.
1st row (WS) Knit.
***With B, work 5" [12.5cm] in stockinette
st, ending with a purl row.
1st and 2nd rows With A, knit.
3rd and 4th rows With B, knit.
Rep last 4 rows of Stripe Pat for 5"
[12.5cm], ending with 2 rows of A.***
Work from *** to *** substituting MC
for A.
Work from *** to *** as given above. Cast off.

FINISHING
Sew strips in the following sequence:
I, II, I, II, I.

Top and bottom edgings With circular
needle and B, pick up and knit 135 sts
across top of Blanket. Do not join in rnd.
Working back and forth across needle, knit
1 row.
****With A, knit 2 rows.
With B, knit 2 rows.
With MC, knit 2 rows.
With B, knit 1 row. Cast off.****
Rep for bottom edge.

Side edgings With circular needle and B,
pick up and knit 163 sts down side of Blanket. Do not join in rnd. Working back and
forth across needle, knit 1 row.
Work from **** to **** as given above.
Rep for other side.

KITTY Blanket

YOU'LL NEED

YARN (3)

Bernat® Baby Sport (12.3oz/350g)
1 ball each
Main Color (MC) (43005 White)
Contrast A (43420 Pink)

NEEDLES

Size 6 (4 mm) knitting needles *or size
to obtain gauge*

MEASUREMENT

Approx 30" [76cm] square.

GAUGE

22 sts and 30 rows = 4" [10cm] in
stockinette st.
Take time to check your gauge.

INSTRUCTIONS

With A, cast on 147 sts.
1st row (RS) K1. *P1. K1. Rep from * to end
of row.
Rep last row of Seed St Pat 7 times more,
ending with a WS row.

Change to MC and proceed as follows
1st row Knit.
2nd and alt rows Purl.
3rd row K7. *K1. K2tog. yo. K1. yo. Sl1. K1.
psso. K8. Rep from * to end of row.
5th row K7. *K2tog. yo. K3. yo. Sl1. K1. psso.
K7. Rep from * to end of row.
7th row K7. *K2. yo. Sl1. K2tog. psso. yo. K9.

Rep from * to end of row.
8th row Purl.
Rep last 8 rows until work from beg measures approx 29" [73.5cm], ending with 8th
row of pat.

Change to A and knit 1 row.
Proceed in Seed St Pat for 7 rows, ending
with a WS row. Cast off in pat.

Side Edging With RS of work facing and A,
beg at lower right corner of blanket, pick
up and knit 155 sts along right side edge.
Work 7 rows in Seed St Pat, ending with RS
facing for next row. Cast off in pat.
Rep for left side edge.

Hood With MC, cast on 43 sts.
1st row (RS) K1. *P1. K1. Rep from * to end
of row.
2nd row K1. *P1. K1. Rep from * to last 2 sts.
P2tog.
3rd row *P1. K1. Rep from * to end of row.
4th row *K1. P1. Rep from * to last 2 sts.
K2tog.
Rep last 4 rows to 2 sts.
Next row K2tog. Fasten off.

Front Edging With RS of work facing and A,
pick up and knit 55 sts across longest side
of triangle.
Work 5 rows in Seed St Pat. Cast off,
sew hood in position to upper left corner
of Blanket, leaving Blanket edging free.

Kitty Ears (make 2)
With A, cast on 6 sts.
1st and alt rows (WS). Purl.
2nd row *K1. (M1. K1) twice. Rep from *

once. 10 sts.
4th row (K1. M1. K3. M1. K1) twice. 14 sts.
6th row (K1. M1. K5. M1. K1) twice. 18 sts.
8th row (K1. M1. K7. M1. K1) twice. 22 sts.
10th row (K1. M1. K9. M1. K1) twice. 26 sts.
12th row (K1. M1. K11. M1. K1) twice. 30 sts.
14th row (K1. M1. K13. M1. K1) twice. 34 sts.
15th row Purl. Break A.
16th row (Picot row) With MC, K2. *yo.
K2tog. Rep from * to end of row.
17th and alt rows Purl.
18th row Kl. (Sl1. K1. psso. K12. K2tog)
twice. K1. 30 sts.
20th row K1.(Sl1. K1. psso. K10. K2tog)
twice. K1. 26 sts.
22nd row K1. (Sl1. K1. psso. K8. K2tog)
twice. K1. 22 sts.
24th row K1. (Sl1. K1. psso. K6. K2tog)
twice. K1. 18 sts.
26th row K1. (Sl1. K1. psso. K4. K2tog)
twice. K1. 14 sts.
28th row K1. (Sl1. K1. psso. K2. K2tog)
twice. K1. 10 sts.
30th row K1. (Sl1. K1. psso. K2tog) twice.
K1. 6 sts.
31st row Purl. Cast off.

FINISHING

Pin Blanket to measurements and cover
with a damp cloth, leaving cloth to dry.
Fold Kitty Ears along Picot row and sew to
Hood of Blanket, having A as inside of ear
as shown in picture.
With A, embroider Kitty's nose using Satin
stitch and whiskers using Chain stitch (see
diagrams).

Chain Stitch

Satin Stitch

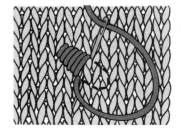

PREEMIE Garter Stitch Set

YOU'LL NEED

YARN ⓷

Bernat® Baby Coordinates (5oz/140g)
Note Amounts are given for Set
(Jacket, Bonnet, Booties and Mittens)
Sizes P3-5 (N5-8, 3, 6, 12, 18)
1 (1-1-1-2-2) balls
(48615 Lemon Custard)

NEEDLES

Size 5 (3.75mm) knitting needles *or
size to obtain gauge.*

ADDITIONAL

4 buttons for jacket
1 button for bonnett
Stitch holder

SIZES

Jacket

To fit chest measurement
Preemie 3-5 lbs 12" [30.5cm]
Newborn 5-8 lbs 14" [35.5cm]
3 mos 16" [40.5cm]
6 mos 17" [43cm]
12 mos 18" [45.5cm]
18 mos 19" [48cm]

Finished chest
Preemie 3-5 lbs 13½" [34.5cm]
Newborn 5-8 lbs 15½" [39.5cm]
3 mos 18" [45.5cm]
6 mos 20" [51cm]
12 mos 21" [53.5cm]
18 mos 22" [56cm]

Bonnet, Booties and Mittens
To fit baby size Preemie (3-6, 12-18) mos.

GAUGE

21 sts and 40 rows = 4" [10cm] in garter st.
Take time to check your gauge.

INSTRUCTIONS

Notes

■ The instructions are written for smallest
size. If changes are necessary for larger

sizes the instructions will be written thus
( ). When only one number is given, it applies to all sizes. For ease in working, circle
all numbers pertaining to your size.
2 Garment is worked side to side in one
piece.

Left Front Cast on 34 (38-43-52-57-64) sts.

Girl's Version only Knit 5 rows (garter st),
noting 1st row is WS.
Boy's Version only Knit 3 rows, noting 1st
row is WS.
Next row (Buttonhole row) K8 (9-11-17-19-
26). [yo. K2tog. K7 (8-9-10-11-11)] twice. yo.
K2tog. K6 (7-8-9-10-10).
Next row Knit.

Both Versions: Shape yoke: **1st row (RS)
K23 (25-28-35-40-45). Turn. Leave rem 11
(13-15-17-17-19) sts unworked.
2nd row K23 (25-28-35-40-45).
3rd and 4th rows Knit to end of row.**
Rep last 4 rows until longer edge (bottom)
from beg measures 4 (4¼-4¾-5¼-5¾-6)"
[10 (11-12-13-14.5-15)cm], ending with a
3rd row. Place marker at beg of last row.

****Sleeve: 1st row (WS)** K16 (18-20-26-28-
30). Leave rem 18 (20-23-26-29-34) sts on
a st holder. Cast on 21 (23-26-28-31-34) sts
for sleeve. 37 (41-46-54-59-64) sts in total.
Next row K26 (28-31-37-42-45). Turn. Leave
rem 11 (13-15-17-17-19) sts unworked.
Next row K21 (23-26-32-37-40). Turn. Leave
rem 5 sts unworked.
Next 2 rows Knit to end of row. 37 (41-46-
54-59-64) sts at end of last row.
Rep last 4 rows 12 (15-18-19-20-20) times
more. [52 (64-76-80-84-84) rows in total].
Next row (RS) Cast off 21 (23-26-28-31-34)
sts. K5 (5-5-9-11-11) (including st on needle
after cast off). Turn. Leave rem
11 (13-15-17-17-19) sts unworked.***
Back: 1st row (WS) K5 (5-5-9-11-11). K18
(20-23-26-29-34) from left front st holder.
Knit 2 rows.
Work from ** to ** as given for Left Front.

Rep last 4 rows until right side from marker
measures 6¾ (7¾-9-10-10½-11)" [17 (19.5-
23-25.5-26.5-28)cm], ending with a 3rd
row. Place marker at beg of last row.
Work from *** to *** as given above.

Right Front: 1st row (WS) K5 (5-5-9-11-11).
K18 (20-23-26-29-34) from back st holder.
Knit 2 rows.
Work from ** to ** as given for Left Front.
Rep last 4 rows until right side from marker
measures 3½ (3¾-4¼-5-5¼-5½)"
[9 (9.5-11-12.5-13-14)cm], ending with a
4th row.

Boy's Version only Knit 5 rows. Cast off.

**Girl's Version only: Next row (Buttonhole
row)** K8 (9-11-17-19-26). [yo. K2tog. K7
(8-9-10-11-11)] twice. yo. K2tog. K6 (7-8-9-
10-10).
Knit 4 rows. Cast off.

FINISHING

Pin garment pieces to measurements.
Cover with a damp cloth, leaving cloth
to dry.

Neck edging With RS of work facing, pick
up and knit 69 (81-90-96-102-108) sts
around neck.
1st row (WS) K6. *K1. K2tog. Rep from * to
last 6 sts. K6. 50 (58-64-68-72-76) sts rem.
2nd row (Buttonhole row) K3. yo. K2tog.
Knit to last 5 sts. K2tog. yo. K3.
Knit 2 rows. Cast off (WS).
Sew sleeve seams.
Sew buttons to correspond to buttonholes.

BONNET

Cast on 26 (31-35) sts.
1st row (RS) K19 (22-25). Turn. Leave rem 7
(9-10) sts unworked.
2nd row K19 (22-25).
3rd and 4th rows Knit to end of row.
Rep last 4 rows until right side from beg
measures 7½ (10-11½)" [19 (25.5-29)cm],
ending with a 3rd row. Cast off.

Neck and chin band Fold 5 sts along front edge to RS and secure at cast on and cast off edges. Thread yarn through each st at shorter edge (back of Bonnet). Pull tightly and secure yarn. With RS of work facing, pick up and knit 37 (42-46) sts along cast on and cast off edges (working through both thicknesses at each end). Cast on 14 sts. 51 (56-60) sts in total.
Knit 1 row.
Next row (Buttonhole row) Knit to last 3 sts. yo. K2tog. K1.
Knit 1 row. Cast off.
Sew button to correspond to buttonhole.

BOOTIES

Cast on 21 (29-33) sts.
1st row (RS) (K1. M1) twice. K7 (11-13). (M1. K1) twice (place marker on last st). M1. K1. M1. K7 (11-13). (M1. K1) twice.
29 (37-41) sts.
2nd row Purl.
3rd row (K1. M1) twice. Knit to 2 sts before marked st. (M1. K1) 3 times. M1. Knit to last 2 sts. (M1. K1) twice.
Rep last 2 rows 0 (0-1) time more. 37 (45-57) sts.
Knit 5 (7-9) rows (garter st).

Shape instep: 1st row K10 (10-12). (K2. ssk) 2 (3-4) times. K1. (K2tog. K2) 2 (3-4) times. K10 (10-12). 33 (39-49) sts rem.
2nd and alt rows Purl.
3rd row K10 (10-12). (K1. ssk) 2 (3-4) times. K1. (K2tog. K1) 2 (3-4) times. K10 (10-12). 29 (33-41) sts rem.
5th row K10 (10-12). (ssk) 2 (3-4) times. K1. (K2tog) 2 (3-4) times. (K2tog) 1 (0-0) time. K8 (10-12). 24 (27-33) sts.
6th row Purl.

Proceed as follows
1st row (RS) *K3. M1. Rep from * to last 3 sts. K3. 31 (35-43) sts.
2nd row P1. *K1. P1. Rep from * to end of row.

3rd row K1. *P1. K1. Rep from * to end of row.
Rep last 2 rows for 2 (3-3)" [5 (7.5-7.5)cm], ending with a WS row. Cast off in rib.
Sew back and sole seam.

MITTENS

Cast on 21 (25-29) sts.
1st row (RS) K1. *P1. K1. Rep from * to end of row.
2nd row P1. *K1. P1. Rep from * to end of row.
Rep last 2 rows for 2" [5cm], ending with a WS row and inc 4 sts evenly across last row. 25 (29-33) sts.
Next row (Eyelets) K1. *yo. K2tog. Rep from * to end of row.
Work in garter st (knit every row) for 1¼" [3cm], ending with a WS row.

Shape top: Next row (RS) K5 (6-7). Sl1. K2tog. psso. K9 (11-13). Sl1. K2tog. psso. K5 (6-7). 21 (25-29) sts rem.
Next row Knit.
Next row K4 (5-6). Sl1. K2tog. psso. K7 (9-11). Sl1. K2tog. psso. K4 (5-6). 17 (21-25) sts rem.
Next row Knit.
Next row K3 (4-5). Sl1. K2tog. psso. K5 (7-9). Sl1. K2tog. psso. K3 (4-5). Cast off. Sew center and top seams.
Cord Cast on 50 sts. Cast off.
Thread through eyelets at wrist.

CHRISTENING Gown

YOU'LL NEED

YARN
Bernat® Baby Coordinates (5oz/140g)
All Sizes Main Color (MC) 2 balls
(48005 White)

NEEDLES
Sizes 3 (3.25mm) and 4 (3.5mm)
knitting needles *or size to obtain gauge.*

ADDITIONAL
2 buttons
3 Stitch holders

◼◼◻◻◻

SIZES
Gown
To fit chest measurement
6 mos 17" [43cm]
12 mos 18" [45.5cm]

MEASUREMENTS
Finished chest
6 mos 19" [48cm]
12 mos 21" [53.5cm]

GAUGE
24 sts and 32 rows = 4" [10cm] with larger
needles in stockinette st.
Take time to check your gauge.

INSTRUCTIONS
Note The instructions are written for smallest size. If changes are necessary for larger
size the instructions will be written thus ( ).
Numbers for each size are shown in the
same color throughout the pattern. When
only one number is given in black, it applies to both sizes.

Panel Pat (worked over 19 sts)
1st row (RS) K2. yo. K4. K2tog. yo. Sl2. K1.
p2sso. yo. ssk. K4. yo. K2.
2nd and alt rows Purl.
3rd row K3. yo. K2. K3tog. yo. K3. yo. Sl1.
K2tog. psso. K2. yo. K3.
5th row K4. yo. K1. K2tog. yo. K1. Sl2. K1.
p2sso. K1. yo. ssk. K1. yo. K4.
7th row K5. yo. K2tog. yo. K1. Sl2. K1. p2sso.
K1. yo. ssk. yo. K5.

9th row K3. K2tog. yo. K1. yo. K2. Sl2. K1.
p2sso. K2. yo. K1. yo. ssk. K3.
11th row K2. K2tog. yo. K3. yo. K1. Sl2. K1.
p2sso. K1. yo. K3. yo. ssk. K2.
13th row K1. K2tog. yo. K5. yo. Sl2. K1.
p2sso. yo. K5. yo. ssk. K1.
14th row Purl.
These 14 rows form Panel Pat.

GOWN
Back
**With larger needles, cast on 156 sts
loosely.

Proceed in Border Pat as follows
1st row (RS) *(K1. yo) twice. Sl1. K2tog.
psso. yo. (K1tbl. P2) 7 times. K1tbl. yo. Sl1.
K2tog. psso. yo. K1. yo. Rep from * to last
st. K1. 166 sts.
2nd row P1. *P6. (K2. P1) 6 times. K2. P7.
Rep from * to end of row.
3rd row *K2. yo. K1. yo. Sl1. K2tog. psso.
yo. (K1tbl. P2) 7 times. K1tbl. yo. Sl1.
K2tog. psso. (yo. K1) twice. Rep from * to
last st. K1. 176 sts.
4th row P1. *P7. (K2. P1) 6 times. K2. P8.
Rep from * to end of row.
5th row *K3. yo. K1. yo. Sl1. K2tog. psso.
yo. (K1tbl. P2) 7 times. K1tbl. yo. Sl1. K2tog.
psso. yo. K1. yo. K2. Rep from * to last st. K1.
186 sts.
6th row P1. *P8. (K2. P1) 6 times. K2. P9. Rep
from * to end of row.
7th row *K4. yo. K1. yo. Sl1. K2tog. psso.
yo. (K1tbl. P2) 7 times. K1tbl. yo. Sl1. K2tog.
psso. yo. K1. yo. K3. Rep from * to last st. K1.
196 sts.
8th row P1. *P9. (K2. P1) 6 times. K2. P10.
Rep from * to end of row.
9th row *K5. yo. K1. yo. Sl1. K2tog. psso.
yo. (K1tbl. P2) 7 times. K1tbl. yo. Sl1. K2tog.
psso. yo. K1. yo. K4. Rep from * to last st. K1.
206 sts.
10th row P1. *P10. (K2. P1) 6 times. K2. P11.
Rep from * to end of row.
11th row *K6. yo. K1. yo. Sl1. K2tog. psso.
yo. (K1tbl. P2) 7 times. K1tbl. yo. Sl1. K2tog.
psso. yo. K1. yo. K5. Rep from * to last st. K1.
216 sts.
12th row P1. *P11. (K2. P1) 6 times. K2. P12.
Rep from * to end of row.
13th row *K7. yo. K1. yo. Sl1. K2tog. psso. yo.

(K1tbl. P2) 7 times. K1tbl. yo. Sl1. K2tog. psso.
yo. K1. yo. K6. Rep from * to last st. K1. 226 sts.
14th row P1. *P12. (K2. P1) 6 times. K2. P13.
Rep from * to end of row.
15th row *K9. yo. Sl1. K2tog. psso. yo. K1.
(K3tog) 7 times. yo. Sl1. K2tog. psso. yo. K8.
Rep from * to last st. K1. 156 sts.

16th row Purl.
These 16 rows form Border Pat.
Rep last 16 rows twice more, dec 1 st at
end of last row. 155 sts.

Proceed in pat as follows
1st row (RS) K6. (Work 1st row Panel Pat.
K12) 4 times. Work 1st row Panel Pat. K6.
2nd row P6. (Work 2nd row Panel Pat. P12)
4 times. Work 2nd row Panel Pat. P6.
Last 2 rows form pat. Panel Pat is now in
position.
Cont in pat, working appropriate rows of
Panel Pat for 26 more rows, ending on a
14th row of Panel Pat.
Next row: Dec row (RS) K2tog. K4. (Work 1st
row Panel Pat. K4. ssk. K2tog. K4) 4 times.
Work 1st row Panel Pat. K4. ssk. 145 sts.
Cont in pat, working appropriate rows of
Panel Pat for 27 more rows, ending on a
14th row of Panel Pat.
Next row: Dec row (RS) K2tog. K3. (Work 1st
row Panel Pat. K3. ssk. K2tog. K3) 4 times.
Work 1st row Panel Pat. K3. ssk. 135 sts.

Cont in pat, working appropriate rows of Panel Pat for 27 more rows, ending on a 14th row of Panel Pat.
Dec row (RS) K2tog. K2. (Work 1st row Panel Pat. K2. ssk. K2tog. K2) 4 times. Work 1st row Panel Pat. K2. ssk. 125 sts.
Cont even in pat, working appropriate rows of Panel Pat until work from beg measures approx 20" [51cm], ending on a 14th row of Panel Pat.

Size 6 mos only: Dec row (RS) *(K2tog) 3 times. K3tog. Rep from * to last 8 sts. (K2. K2tog) twice. 58 sts.
Size 12 mos only: Next row: Dec row (RS) K1. *K2tog. Rep from * to last 2 sts. K2. 64 sts.
Both sizes: Next row Purl.

Shape armholes Cast off 4 sts beg next 2 rows. Dec 1 st each end of needle on next row and every following alt row 3 times more. 42 (48) sts rem.**
Next row Purl.

Divide for back opening: Next row (RS) K21 (24) for neck edge. Turn. Leave rem sts on a spare needle.
Cont even in stockinette st until armhole measures 4 (4½)" [10 (11.5)cm], ending with a purl row.

Shape shoulder Cast off 4 (5) sts beg next and following alt row. Leave rem 13 (14) sts on a st holder.

With RS facing, join yarn to rem 21 (24) sts. Cont even in stockinette st until armhole measures 4 (4½)" [10 (11.5)cm], ending with a knit row.

Shape shoulder Cast off 4 (5) sts beg next and following alt row. Leave rem 13 (14) sts on a st holder.

Front
Work from ** to ** as given for Back. Cont even in stockinette st until armhole measures 2 (2½)" [5 (6)cm], ending with a purl row.

Shape neck: Next row (RS) K15 (17) (neck edge). Turn. Leave rem sts on a spare needle.
Dec 1 st at neck edge on next 4 rows, then on every following alt row 3 times. 8 (10) sts rem.
Cont even until armhole measures same length as Back to beg of shoulder shaping, ending with a purl row.

Shape shoulder Cast off 4 (5) sts beg next row. Purl 1 row. Cast off rem 4 (5) sts.
With RS facing, slip next 12 (14) sts onto a st holder. Join yarn to rem sts and knit to end of row.
Dec 1 st at neck edge on next 4 rows, then on every following alt row 3 times. 8 (10) sts rem.

Cont even until armhole measures same length as Back to beg of shoulder shaping, ending with a knit row.

Shape shoulder Cast off 4 (5) sts beg next row. Knit 1 row. Cast off rem 4 (5) sts.

Sleeves
With larger needles, cast on 59 (62) sts.
1st row (WS) Knit.
2nd row P2. *K1tbl. P2. Rep from * to end of row.
3rd row K2. *P1. K2. Rep from * to end of row.
4th to 9th rows Rep 2nd and 3rd rows 3 times more.
10th row K3. (K3tog) 18 (19) times. K2. 23 (24) sts.
11th row *Inc 1 st in next st purlwise. Rep from * to end of row. 46 (48) sts.
Beg with a knit row, cont in stockinette st for 6 more rows.

Shape top Cast off 2 sts beg next 2 rows. Dec 1 st at each end of next row and every following alt row until there are 24 sts, then on every row until there are 14 sts. Cast off.

FINISHING
Pin garment pieces to measurements. Cover with a damp cloth, leaving cloth to dry. Sew shoulder seams.

Neckband With RS facing and smaller needles, K13 (14) from left back st holder. Pick up and knit 13 sts down left front neck edge. K12 (14) from front st holder. Pick up and knit 13 sts up right front neck edge. K13 (14) from right back st holder. 64 (68) sts.
Knit 4 rows (garter st). Cast off knitwise.
Back edging With RS facing and smaller needles, pick up and knit 23 (25) sts down right back opening and 23 (25) sts up left back opening. 46 (50) sts.
Next row K2. Cast off 2 sts. K13. Cast off 2 sts. Knit to end of row.
Next row Knit, casting on 2 sts over cast off sts. Cast off knitwise.
Sew side and sleeve seams. Sew in sleeves. Sew on buttons to correspond to buttonholes.

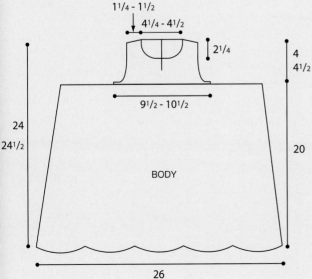

1¼ - 1½
4¼ - 4½
2¼
9½ - 10½
4
4½
24
24½
20
BODY

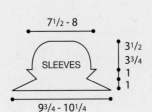

7½ - 8
3½
3¾
1
1
SLEEVES
9¾ - 10¼
26

CHRISTENING Blanket

YOU'LL NEED

YARN 🔢3

Bernat® Baby Coordinates(5oz/140g)
Main Color (MC) 4 balls (48005 White)

NEEDLES

Size 6 (4mm) knitting needles. Size 6 (4mm) circular knitting needle 36" [90cm] long *or size to obtain gauge*

SIZE

Approx 45" [114.5cm] square.

GAUGE

22 sts and 30 rows = 4" [10cm] in stockinette st.
Take time to check your gauge.

INSTRUCTIONS

Note The instructions are written for smallest size. If changes are necessary for larger size the instructions will be written thus ( ). Numbers for each size are shown in the same color throughout the pattern. When only one number is given in black, it applies to both sizes.

Panel Pat (worked over 19 sts)
1st row (RS) K2. yo. K4. K2tog. yo. Sl2. K1. p2sso. yo. ssk. K4. yo. K2.
2nd and alt rows Purl.
3rd row K3. yo. K2. K3tog. yo. K3. yo. Sl1. K2tog. psso. K2. yo. K3.
5th row K4. yo. K1. K2tog. yo. K1. Sl2. K1. p2sso. K1. yo. ssk. K1. yo. K4.
7th row K5. yo. K2tog. yo. K1. Sl2. K1. p2sso. K1. yo. ssk. yo. K5.
9th row K3. K2tog. yo. K1. yo. K2. Sl2. K1. p2sso. K2. yo. K1. yo. ssk. K3.
11th row K2. K2tog. yo. K3. yo. K1. Sl2. K1. p2sso. K1. yo. K3. yo. ssk. K2.
13th row K1. K2tog. yo. K5. yo. Sl2. K1. p2sso. yo. K5. yo. ssk. K1.
14th row Purl.
These 14 rows form Panel Pat.

BLANKET

Center Section Cast on 197 sts. Do not join. Working back and forth across needle in rows, proceed as follows
1st row (RS) K5. (Work 1st row Panel Pat. K9) 6 times. Work 1st row Panel Pat. K5.
2nd row P5. (Work 2nd row Panel Pat. P9) 6 times. Work 2nd row Panel Pat. P5.
Last 2 rows form pat. Panel Pat is now in position.
Cont in pat, working appropriate rows of Panel Pat until work from beg measures approx 36" [91.5cm], ending on a 14th row of Panel Pat. Cast off loosely.

Side Sections (make 4)

Cast on 259 sts. Do not join. Working back and forth across needle in rows, proceed as follows
1st row (RS) K1. yo. Sl1. K2tog. psso. K32. *(K1. yo) twice. Sl1. K2tog. psso. yo. (K1tbl. P2) 7 times. K1tbl. yo. Sl1. K2tog. psso. yo. K1. yo.* Rep from * to * 5 times more. K33. Sl1. K2tog. psso. yo. K1.
2nd row K36. *K5. P1. (K2. P1) 7 times. K6.* Rep from * to * 5 times more. K35.
3rd row K1. yo. Sl1. K2tog. psso. K31. *K2. yo. K1. yo. Sl1. K2tog. psso. yo. (K1tbl. P2) 7 times. K1tbl. yo. Sl1. K2tog. psso. (yo. K1) twice.* Rep from * to * 5 times more. K32. Sl1. K2tog. psso. yo. K1.
4th row K2. K2tog. K31. *K6. P1. (K2. P1) 7 times. K7.* Rep from * to * 5 times more. K30. K2tog. K2.
5th row K1. yo. K2tog. K30. *K3. yo. K1. yo. Sl1. K2tog. psso. yo. (K1tbl. P2) 7 times. K1tbl. yo. Sl1. K2tog. psso. yo. K1. yo. K2.* Rep from * to * 5 times more. K31. K2tog. yo. K1.
6th row K2. K2tog. K30. *K7. P1. (K2. P1) 7 times. K8.* Rep from * to * 5 times more. K29. K2tog. K2.
7th row K1. yo. Sl1. K2tog. psso. K28. *K4. yo. K1. yo. Sl1. K2tog. psso. yo. (K1tbl. P2) 7 times. K1tbl. yo. Sl1. K2tog. psso. yo. K1. yo. K3.* Rep from * to * 5 times more. K29. Sl1. K2tog. psso. yo. K1.

8th row K32. *K8. P1. (K2. P1) 7 times. K9.* Rep from * to * 5 times more. K31.
9th row K1. yo. Sl1. K2tog. psso. K27. *K5. yo. K1. yo. Sl1. K2tog. psso. yo. (K1tbl. P2) 7 times. K1tbl. yo. Sl1. K2tog. psso. yo. K1. K4.* Rep from * to * 5 times more. K28. Sl1 K2tog. psso. yo. K1.
10th row K2. K2tog. K27. *K9. P1. (K2. P1) 7 times. K10.* Rep from * to * 5 times more. K26. K2tog. K2.
11th row K1. yo. K2tog. K26. *K6. yo. K1. yo. Sl1. K2tog. psso. yo. (K1tbl. P2) 7 times. K1tbl. yo. Sl1. K2tog. psso. yo. K1. yo. K5.* Rep from * to * 5 times more. K27. K2tog. yo. K1.
12th row K2. K2tog. K26. *K10. P1. (K2. P1) times. K11.* Rep from * to * 5 times more. K25. K2tog. K2.
13th row K1. yo. Sl1. K2tog. psso. K24. *K7. yo. K1. yo. Sl1. K2tog. psso. yo. (K1tbl. P2) 7 times. K1tbl. yo. Sl1. K2tog. psso. yo. K1. yo. K6.* Rep from * to * 5 times more. K25. Sl1 K2tog. psso. yo. K1.
14th row K28. *K11. P1. (K2. P1) 7 times. K12.* Rep from * to * 5 times more. K27.
15th row K1. yo. Sl1. K2tog. psso. K23. Place marker. *K9. yo. Sl1. K2tog. psso. yo. K1. (K3tog) 7 times. yo. Sl1. K2tog. psso. yo. K8 Rep from * to * 5 times more. Place marke K24. Sl1. K2tog. psso. yo. K1.
16th row K2. K2tog. Knit to last 4 sts. K2tog K2.
Last 16 rows form 6 reps of pat between markers.
Work a further 16 rows in pat, dec 1 st at each end of every row (as before). 205 sts rem. Cast off loosely.

FINISHING

Block all pieces to measurements. Cover with a damp cloth and allow cloth to dry. Sew cast off edges of Side Sections to side edges of Center Section. Sew mitered seams at corners.

PRETTY IN Pink Set

SIZES

Cardigan

To fit chest measurement
6 mos 17" [43cm]
12 mos 19" [48cm]
18 mos 21" [53.5cm]

Finished chest
6 mos 20" [51cm]
12 mos 21½" [54.5cm]
18 mos 23½" [59.5cm]

Cap sized for 6 mos or 12-18 mos.

GAUGE

22 sts and 30 rows = 4" [10cm] in
stockinette st.
Take time to check your gauge.

INSTRUCTIONS

Note The instructions are written for smallest size. If changes are necessary for larger
sizes the instructions will be written thus
( ). When only one number is given, it applies to all sizes. For ease in working, circle
all numbers pertaining to your size.

BODY

Note Body is worked in one piece to armholes.

First Motif
With crochet hook, ch 4. Join with
sl st to first ch to form ring.
1st rnd Ch 3. 1 dc in ring – counts as
dc2tog. Ch 2. (Yo and draw up a loop in
ring. Yo and draw through 2 loops on
hook) twice. Yo and draw through all loops
on hook - dc2tog made. (Ch 2. Dc2tog) 6
times. Ch 2. Sl st to top of ch 3.
2nd rnd Ch 1. 1 sc in same sp as last sl st.
*Ch 5. 1 sc in next dc2tog. Ch 3. 1 sc in
next dc2tog. Rep from * twice more. Ch
5. 1 sc in next dc2tog. Ch 3. Sl st in first sc.
Fasten off.

Next 10 (11-12) Motifs
1st rnd Work as given for 1st rnd of First
Motif.
2nd rnd Ch 1. 1 sc in same sp as last sl st.
Ch 5. 1 sc in next dc2tog. Ch 3. 1 sc in next
dc2tog. Ch 2. Sl st in corner of adjoining
Motif. Ch 2. 1 sc in next dc2tog. Ch 1. Sl
st in ch-3 sp of adjoining Motif. Ch 1. 1
sc in next dc2tog. Ch 2. Sl st in corner of
adjoining Motif. Ch 2. 1 sc in next dc2tog.
Ch 3. 1 sc in next dc2tog. Ch 5. 1 sc in next
dc2tog. Ch 3. Sl st in first sc. Fasten off.

With RS of work facing, join yarn with sl
st to top right corner of Motifs strip. Work
8 sc across top of first Motif. *Work 1 sc
in joining sp between 2 Motifs. Work 9 sc
across top of next Motif. Rep from * across,
ending with 8 sc across top of last Motif.
107 (117-127) sc. Fasten off.

With RS of work facing and knitting
needles, pick up and knit 1 st in each sc
across last row. 107 (117-127) sts.
Beg with a purl row, cont in stockinette
st until work from bottom edge of Motifs
measures 5½ (6-7)" [14 (15-18)cm], ending
with RS facing for next row.

Divide for armholes: Next row K23 (25-
26). Cast off next 6 (8-10) sts. K49 (51-55)
(including st on needle after cast off). Cast
off next 6 (8-10) sts. Knit to end of row.
Cont on last 23 (25-26) sts for Left Front.
Purl 1 row.

Dec 1 st at armhole edge on next and
following alt row(s) 1 (1-2) time(s) more. 21
(23-23) sts.
Cont even until armhole measures 2¼ (2½-
3)" [5.5 (6-7.5)cm], ending with WS facing
for next row.

Shape neck: Next row Cast off 5 (6-5) sts.
Purl to end of row.
Dec 1 st at neck edge on next and following
alt rows 3 (4-4) times more. 12 (12-13) sts.
Work 3 rows even, ending with RS facing
for next row.

Shape shoulder Cast off 6 sts beg next row.
Work 1 row even. Cast off rem 6 (6-7) sts.

With WS of work facing, join yarn to center
49 (51-55) sts (Back).
Purl 1 row.
Dec 1 st each end of needle on next and
following alt row(s) 1 (1-2) time(s) more.
45 (47-49) sts.
Cont even until armhole measures 4 rows
less than Left Front to beg of shoulder
shaping.

Shape neck: Next row (RS) K15 (15-16).
Cast off next 15 (17-17) sts. Knit to end of row.
Cont on last 15 (15-16) sts.
Dec 1 st at neck edge on next 3 rows. 12
(12-13) sts.
Knit 1 row.

Shape shoulder Cast off 6 sts beg next row.
Work 1 row even. Cast off rem 6 (6-7) sts.

With WS of work facing, join yarn to rem 15
(15-16) sts.
Dec 1 st at neck edge on next 3 rows. 12
(12-13) sts.

Shape shoulder Cast off 6 sts beg next row.
Work 1 row even. Cast off rem 6 (6-7) sts.

With WS of work facing, join yarn to last 23
(25-26) sts for Right Front. Work as given
for Left Front reversing all shapings.

SLEEVES

Work 4 Motifs as given for Body.
With RS of work facing, join yarn with sl st to top right corner of Motifs strip. Work 9 sc across top of first Motif. (Work 1 sc in joining sp between 2 Motifs. Work 9 sc across top of next Motif) 3 times. 39 sc. Fasten off.

With RS of work facing and larger knitting needles, pick up and knit 1 st in each sc across last row. 39 sts.
Beg with a purl row, cont in stockinette st for 7 more rows.
Inc 1 st each end of needle on next and following 10th (6th-6th) rows until there are 43 (47-49) sts.

Cont even until work from bottom edge of Motifs measures 5 (6-7½)" [12.5 (15-19) cm], ending with RS facing for next row.

Shape top Cast off 2 (2-3) sts beg next 2 rows. 39 (43-43) sts.
Dec 1 st each end of needle on next and following alt rows until there are 27 (29-25) sts, then on every row until there are 9 (11-11) sts. Cast off.
Sew sleeve seams.

Sleeve Edging With RS of work facing and crochet hook, join yarn with sl st to bottom right corner of Motifs. Work 37 sc across bottom edge of Motifs. Join with sl st in first sc.
Next rnd Ch 1. 1 sc in first sc. *Skip next 2 sc. 5 dc in next sc. Skip next 2 sc. 1 sc in last sc. Rep from * across. Join with sl st in first sc. Fasten off.

FINISHING

Sew in sleeves.
Edging: 1st rnd With RS of work facing, join yarn with crochet hook to lower corner of Right Front.
Ch 1. 1 sc in same sp. Work a further 43 (49-53) sc up Right Front edge to top corner, 57 (63-69) sc around neck edge, 44 (50-54) sc down Left Front edge to lower corner and 110 (122-134) sc across bottom edge to opposite corner. Join with sl st to first sc. 198 (222-240) sc.
2nd rnd Ch 3. 2 dc in same sp as last sl st. *Skip next 2 sc. 1 sc in next sc. Skip next 2 sc. 5 dc in next sc. Rep from * around, ending with 2 dc in same sp as first 2 dc. Join with sl st to top of ch 3. Fasten off.
Sew button to Left Front using edging to create buttonhole at neck edge.

PANTS
Right Leg
Beg at waist, with MC and smaller needles cast on 53 (55-61) sts.
Work 14 rows in stockinette st.

Change to larger needles and proceed as follows
1st row (RS) Knit.
2nd row P35 (40-45). Turn.
Leave rem sts unworked.
3rd and alt rows Knit.
4th row P25 (30-35). Turn.
Leave rem sts unworked.
6th row P15 (20-25). Turn.
Leave rem sts unworked.
8th row Purl across all sts. Place a marker at end of last row.
**Cont even in stockinette st until work from marker measures 4 (4-4½)" [10 (10-11.5)cm], ending with RS facing for next row.

Shape crotch Inc 1 st each end of needle on next and following alt rows 3 times. 61 (63-69) sts. Cast on 4 sts beg next 2 rows. 69 (71-77) sts.
Place a 2nd marker at end of last row.
Work 4 rows even.

Shape inseam Dec 1 st each end of needle on next and following 4th (4th-8th) rows until there are 59 (61-69) sts.

Cont even until work from 2nd marker measures 3½ (4-5)" [9 (10-12.5)cm], ending with RS facing for next row. Cast off.

Motif Edging Work 6 (6-7) Motifs as given for Body.
With RS of work facing, join yarn with sl st to top right corner of Motifs strip. Work 9

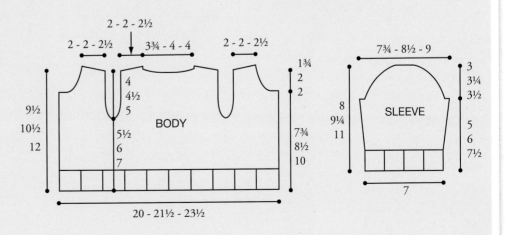

sc across top of first Motif. *Work 1 sc in joining sp between 2 Motifs. Work 9 sc across top of next Motif. Rep from * across. 59 (59-69) sc. Fasten off.

Bottom Edging With RS of work facing and crochet hook, join yarn with sl st to bottom right corner of Motifs. Work 55 (55-67) sc across bottom edge of Motifs. Fasten off.
Next row With RS of work facing, join yarn with sl st to first sc of last row. Ch 1. 1 sc in same sc. *Skip next 2 sc. 5 dc in next sc. Skip next 2 sc. 1 sc in last sc. Rep from * across. Fasten off.

With RS facing each other, place top edge of Motifs along cast off edge of Leg. With crochet hook, work 1 row of sc through both thicknesses to join.**

Left Leg
Beg at waist, with smaller needles cast on 53 (55-61) sts.
Work 14 rows in stockinette st.

Change to larger needles and proceed as follows
1st row K35 (40-45). Turn.
Leave rem sts unworked.
2nd and alt rows Purl.
3rd row K25 (30-35). Turn.
Leave rem sts unworked.
5th row K15 (20-25). Turn.
Leave rem sts unworked.
7th row Knit across all sts. Place a marker at end of last row.

Work from ** to ** as given for Right Leg.

FINISHING
Sew inseams. Sew crotch seam. Fold waistband in half to WS and sew in position leaving an opening at center back to insert elastic. Cut elastic to waist measurement and draw through waistband. Sew ends of elastic tog securely. Sew opening closed.

CAP
Motif Edging Work 10 Motifs as given for Body.

Size 6 mos only With RS of work facing and

crochet hook, join yarn with sl st to top right corner of Motifs strip. Work 8 sc across top of first Motif. *Work 1 sc in joining sp between 2 Motifs. Work 9 sc across top of next Motif. Rep from * across, ending with 8 sc across top of last Motif. 97 sc.

Size 12-18 mos only With RS of work facing and crochet hook, join yarn with sl st to top right corner of Motifs strip. Work 9 sc across top of first Motif. (Work 1 sc in joining sp between 2 Motifs. Work 9 sc across top of next Motif) 5 times. (Work 1 sc in joining sp between 2 Motifs. Work 10 sc across top of next Motif) 4 times. 103 sc.

Both sizes With RS of work facing and crochet hook, join yarn with sl st to bottom right corner of Motifs. Work 97 (103) sc across bottom edge of Motifs as given above. Fasten off.
Next row With RS of work facing, join yarn with sl st to first sc of last row. Ch 1. 1 sc in same sc. *Skip next 2 sc. 5 dc in next sc. Skip next 2 sc. 1 sc in next sc. Rep from * across. Fasten off.

Top of Cap With RS of work facing and larger knitting needles, pick up and knit 1 st in each sc across top edge of Motifs. 97 (103) sts.
Beg with a purl row, cont in stockinette st until work from bottom edge of Motifs measures 4 (4½)" [10 (11.5)cm], ending with a purl row.

Shape top: 1st row K1. *K2tog. K14 (15). Rep from * to end of row. 91 (97) sts.
2nd and alt rows Purl.
3rd row K1. *K2tog. K13 (14). Rep from * to end of row. 85 (91) sts.
5th row K1. *K2tog. K12 (13). Rep from * to end of row. 79 (85) sts.
6th row Purl.
Cont in this manner, dec 6 sts evenly across next and following alt rows, until there are 61 sts.
Next row (WS) (P8. P2tog) 6 times. P1. 55 sts.
Next row K1. (K2tog. K7) 6 times. 49 sts.
Cont in this manner, dec 6 sts evenly across next and every following row until there are 25 sts.

Next row (RS) (K1. K2tog) 8 times. K1. 17 sts. Break yarn leaving a long end. Draw end through rem sts and fasten securely. Sew center back seam.

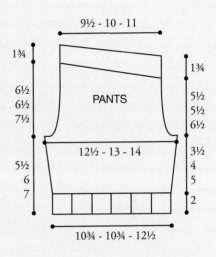

EASY AS PIE Blanket

YOU'LL NEED

YARN
Bernat® Baby Sport (12.3oz/350g)

1 ball each
Pink and White Version
Main Color (MC) (43420 Pink)
Contrast A (43005 White)

Green and Blue Version
Main Color (MC) (43230 Mint)
Contrast A (43128 Pale Blue)

NEEDLES
Size 6 (4mm) circular knitting needle 24"
[60cm] long *or size to obtain gauge*

ADDITIONAL
Size U.S. D or 3 (3.25mm) crochet hook

MEASUREMENTS
Approx 27½ x 32½" [70 x 82.5cm].

GAUGE
18 sts and 40 rows = 4" [10cm] in garter st.
Motif = 2½" [6cm] square.
Take time to check your gauge.

INSTRUCTIONS

Center Section
With MC, cast on 100 sts. Do not join.
Working back and forth across needle
in rows, proceed in garter st (knit every
row), until work from beg measures 27"
[68.5cm]. Cast off.

Motif I (make 18)
With MC and crochet hook, ch 4. Join with
sl st to form a ring.
1st rnd Ch 3 (counts as dc). 2 dc in ring. (Ch
2. 3 dc) 3 times in ring.
Ch 2. Join with sl st to top of ch 3. Fasten
off.
2nd rnd Join A with sl st to any corner. Ch
3 (counts as dc). (2 dc. Ch 2. 3 dc) in same
sp. [Ch 1. (3 dc. Ch 2. 3 dc) in next ch-2 sp]
3 times. Ch 1. Join with sl st to top of ch 3.
Fasten off.
3rd rnd Join MC with sl st to any corner. Ch
3 (counts as dc). (2 dc. Ch 2. 3 dc) in same
sp. Ch 1. 3 dc in next ch-1 sp. Ch 1. [(3 dc.
Ch 2. 3 dc) in next ch-2 sp. Ch 1. 3 dc in
next ch-1 sp. Ch 1] 3 times. Join with sl st
to top of ch 3. Fasten off.

Motif II (make 18)
Work as given for Motif I, substituting A for
MC and MC for A.

FINISHING
Block Center Section to measure
21 x 27" [53.5 x 68.5cm].

Sew 9 motifs tog,
alternating Motif I
and Motif II, across
top and bottom and
11 motifs tog, alter-
nating Motif II and
Motif I, for sides. Do
not sew to blanket.
Proceed as follows

Inner Edging Join MC
with sl st to first Motif
of bottom left corner
to inside of Granny
Square border.
Ch 1. *Work 1 sc in
each of next 9 dc
across first Motif.
Work 1 sc in joining
sp between 2 Motifs.
Rep from * to next
corner of Border. Dec
in corner as follows
Draw up loop in cor-
ner 2 dc. Yo and draw
through all 3 loops
on hook - Sc2tog

made.** Rep from * to ** around, working
sc2tog across last and first sc. Join with sl st
to first sc. Fasten off.

Outer Edging Join MC with sl st to any
corner. Ch 1. Work 1 sc in each of next 9 dc
across first Motif.*
Work 1 sc in joining sp between 2 Motifs.
Work 1 sc in each of next 9 dc across next
Motif. Rep from * around, working 3 sc in
corners. Join with sl st to first sc. Fasten off.

Sew Granny Square border to Center Section of Blanket.

PREPPY BOY'S Vest

YOU'LL NEED

YARN
Bernat® Baby Sport (12.3oz/350g)
All Sizes 1 ball each
Main Color (MC) (43128 Pale Blue)
Contrast A (43230 Mint)

NEEDLES
Sizes 4 (3.5mm) and 6 (4mm) knitting
needles. Size 4 (3.5mm) circular knitting
needle 24" [60cm] long
or size to obtain gauge

SIZES
To fit chest measurement
3 mos 16" [40.5cm]
6 mos 17" [43cm]
12 mos 19" [48cm]
18 mos 21" [53.5cm]

Finished chest
3 mos 19½" [49.5cm]
6 mos 21" [53.5cm]
12 mos 24" [61cm]
18 mos 25" [63.5cm]

GAUGE
22 sts and 30 rows = 4" [10cm] with larger
needles in stockinette st.
Take time to check your gauge.

INSTRUCTIONS
Note The instructions are written for
smallest size. If changes are necessary for
larger sizes the instructions will be written
thus ( ). When only one number is given,
it applies to all sizes. For ease in working,
circle all numbers pertaining to your size.

FRONT
**With MC and smaller needles, cast on 50
(54-62-66) sts.
1st row (RS) K2. *P2. K2. Rep from * to end
of row.
2nd row P2. *K2. P2. Rep from * to end of
row.

Rep last 2 rows 3 times more, inc 4 sts
evenly across last row. 54 (58-66-70) sts.
Change to larger needles and cont in
stockinette st until work from beg measures 3¾ (4¾-5¼-6)" [9.5 (12-13-15)cm],
ending with RS facing for next row.

Proceed in Stripe pat as follows :
With A, work 4 rows in stockinette st.
With MC, work 2 rows in stockinette st.
Next row (RS) With MC, K2. *With A, K2.
With MC, K2. Rep from * to end of row.
With MC, beg with purl row, work 2 rows in
stockinette st.
With A, beg with purl row, work 4 rows in
stockinette st.
Next row (WS) With MC, purl.

Shape armholes With MC, cast off 4 (4-5-5)
sts beg next 2 rows. 46 (50-56-60) sts.
Dec 1 st each end of needle on next and
following alt row(s) 1 (1-2-3) time(s) more.
42 (46-50-52) sts.**
Purl 1 row.

V-Neck shaping: Next row (RS) K21 (23-25-
26). Turn. Leave rem sts on a spare needle.
Next row Purl.
Next row Knit to last 4 sts. K2tog. K2.
Next row Purl.
Rep last 2 rows 9 (7-8-7) times more. 11
(15-16-18) sts.

Sizes 6, 12 and 18 mos only
Next row (RS) Knit to last 4 sts.
K2tog. K2.
Work 3 rows even in stockinette
st.
Rep last 4 rows (1-1-2) time(s)
more. (13-14-15) sts.

All sizes: Shape shoulder Cast
off 6 (6-7-7) sts beg of next row.
Work 1 row even. Cast off rem 5
(7-7-8) sts.

With RS of work facing, join MC
to rem sts. Knit to end of row.

Next row Purl.
Next row (RS) K2. Sl1. K1. psso. Knit to end
of row.
Next row Purl.
Rep last 2 rows 9 (7-8-7) times more. 11
(15-16-18) sts.

Sizes 6, 12 and 18 mos only: Next row (RS)
K2. Sl1. K1. psso. Knit to end of row.
Work 3 rows even in stockinette st.
Rep last 4 rows (1-1-2) time(s) more. (13-
14-15) sts.

All sizes: Next row (RS) Knit.

Shape shoulder Cast off 6 (6-7-7) sts beg of
next row. Work 1 row even. Cast off rem 5
(7-7-8) sts.

BACK
Work from ** to ** as given for Front.
Work even in stockinette st until armhole
measures same length as Front to beg of
shoulder shaping, ending with a purl row.

Shape shoulders Cast off 6 (6-7-7) sts beg
next 2 rows, then cast off 5 (7-7-8) sts beg
following 2 rows. Leave rem 20 (20-22-22)
sts on a st holder.

FINISHING

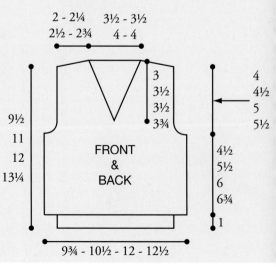

Neckband Sew shoulder seams. With RS of work facing, circular needle and MC, pick up and knit 29 (29-32-32) sts up Right Front V-neck edge. K20 (20-22-22) from back neck st holder. Pick up and knit 29 (29-32-32) sts down Left Front V-neck edge. 78 (78-86-86) sts. Do not join. Working back and forth across needle in rows, proceed as follows

2nd row (WS) P2. *K2. P2. Rep from * to end of row.

3rd row K2. *P2. K2. Rep from * to end of row.

Rep last 2 rows once more, then 2nd row once. Cast off in ribbing.

Sew sides of neckband in position, lapping left side over right side.

Armbands With RS of work facing, MC and smaller needles, pick up and knit 61 (61-67-73) sts evenly along armhole edge.

Knit 2 rows. Cast off knitwise (WS). Sew side and armband seams.

RUFFLE Edge Blanket

YOU'LL NEED

YARN
Bernat® Big Ball Baby Sport
(12.3oz/350g)
Contrast A 1 ball (21420 Baby Pink)

NEEDLES
Size 6 (4mm) circular knitting needle
36" [90cm] long *or size to obtain gauge*

GAUGE
22 sts and 28 rows = 4" [10cm] in stockinette st.
Take time to check your gauge.

MEASUREMENT
Approx 36" [91.5cm] square.

INSTRUCTIONS

Blanket
Cast on 162 sts. Do not join. Working back and forth across needle in rows, purl 1 row.
1st row (RS) K1. *yo. K2tog. K3. ssk. yo. K1. Rep from * to last st. K1.
2nd and alt rows Purl.
3rd row K1. *K1. yo. K2tog. K1. ssk. yo. K2. Rep from * to last st. K1.
5th row Knit.
7th row K1. *K1. ssk. yo. K1. yo. K2tog. K2. Rep from * to last st. K1.
9th row K1. *ssk. yo. K3. yo. K2tog. K1. Rep from * to last st. K1.
11th row Knit.
12th row As 2nd row.
These 12 rows form Lace Pat (see chart).
Cont in pat until work from beg measures 32" [81.5cm], ending with a WS row.
Cast off.

Ruffle Border
With RS facing, pick up and knit 162 sts across top edge. Do not join in rnd. Working back and forth across needle, knit 3 rows (garter st).
1st row (RS) K1. *K1. P7. Rep from * to last st. K1.
2nd row K1. *K7. P1. Rep from * to last st. K1.
3rd row K1. *yo. K1. yo. P7. Rep from * to last st. K1.
4th row K1. *K7. P2. P1tbl. Rep from * to last st. K1.
5th row K1. *yo. K3. yo. P7. Rep from * to last st. K1.
6th row K1. *K7. P4. P1tbl. Rep from * to last st. K1.
7th row K1. *yo. K5. yo. P7. Rep from * to last st. K1.
8th row K1. *K7. P6. P1tbl. Rep from * to last st. K1.
9th row K1. *yo. K7. yo. P7. Rep from * to last st. K1.
10th row K1. *K7. P8. P1tbl. Rep from * to last st. K1.
11th row K1. *yo. K9. yo. P7. Rep from * to last st. K1.
12th row K1. *K7. P10. P1tbl. Rep from * to last st. K1.
Cast off. Rep for 3 rem edges.
Sew short sides of Ruffle Border tog at corners.

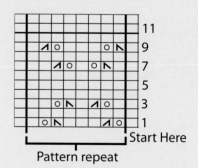

Start Here

Pattern repeat

□ = Knit on RS rows. Purl on WS rows

◩ = K2tog

◨ = Ssk

◻ = Yo

GIRLIE Monster

GAUGE
25 sts and 31 rows = 4" [10cm] in stockinette st.
Take time to check your gauge.

MEASUREMENT
Approx 9" [23cm] tall, excluding legs and ears.

INSTRUCTIONS
Monster Body
With double-pointed needles and A, cast on 6 sts. Divide sts onto 3 needles (2 sts on each needle). Join in rnd.

Proceed in Stripe Pat as follows
**1st rnd (Inc 1 st in next st) 6 times. 12 sts.
2nd and alt rnds Knit.
3rd rnd (Inc 1 st in next st. K1) 6 times. 18 sts.***
5th rnd (Inc 1 st in next st. K2) 6 times. 24 sts.
7th rnd With B, (Inc 1 st in next st. K3) 6 times. 30 sts.
9th rnd (Inc 1 st in next st. K4) 6 times. 36 sts.**
11th rnd (Inc 1 st in next st. K5) 6 times. 42 sts.
12th rnd With B, as 2nd rnd.
First 12 rnds of Stripe Pat (6 rnds of A, 6 rnds of B) are completed.
Cont in same manner, keeping cont of Stripe Pat, inc 6 sts on next and every following alt rnd until there are 102 sts. Place marker at end of last rnd.
Cont even in rnds until work from marked rnd measures 5" [12.5cm].

Shape top Keeping cont of Stripe Pat, proceed as follows
1st rnd (K15. K2tog) 6 times. K1. 96 sts.
2nd and alt rnds Purl.
3rd rnd (K14. K2tog) 6 times. 90 sts.
5th rnd (K13. K2tog) 6 times. 84 sts.
7th rnd (K12. K2tog) 6 times. 78 sts.
9th rnd (K11. K2tog) 6 times. 72 sts.
Stuff Body.
11th rnd (K10. K2tog) 6 times. 66 sts.
13th rnd (K9. K2tog) 6 times. 60 sts.
Cont in same manner, dec 6 sts on every following alt rnd until there are 6 sts.

Break yarn leaving a long end. Draw end tightly through rem sts and fasten securely.

Legs (make 2)
Foot With B, work from ** to ** as given for Body.
Knit 6 rnds.
1st rnd (K2tog. K4) 6 times. 30 sts.
2nd and alt rnds Knit.
3rd rnd (K2tog. K3) 6 times. 24 sts.
5th rnd (K2tog. K2) 6 times. 18 sts.
7th rnd (K2tog. K1) 6 times. 12 sts. Break B.
Stuff Foot.
With A, knit in rnds for 4" [10cm].
Cast off. Do not stuff A section.
Sew Legs in position.

Nose
With B, work from ** to *** as given for Body.
Knit 6 rnds. Cast off.
Stuff Nose and sew in position.

Ears (make 2)
With pair of needles and A, cast on 5 sts.
1st row (RS) K2. yo. K1. yo. K2.
2nd and alt rows Knit.
3rd row K3. yo. K1. yo. K3.
5th row K4. yo. K1. yo. K4.
7th row K5. yo. K1. yo. K5.
9th row K6. yo. K1. yo. K6.
11th row K7. yo. K1. yo. K7.
13th row K8. yo. K1. yo. K8.
15th row K7. K2tog. yo. K1. yo. ssk. K7.
16th row Knit.
Rep last 2 rows twice more.
Next row (RS) K2tog. Knit to last 2 sts. ssk.
Next row Knit.
Rep last 2 rows until there are 3 sts.
Next row (RS) Sl1. K2tog. psso. Fasten off.

Sew Ears in position. With black yarn, embroider eyes using satin stitch, and eyelashes using straight stitch.

Skirt
With pair of needles and A, cast on 105 sts.
1st row (RS) K1. *K1. P7. Rep from * to end of row.
2nd row *K7. P1. Rep from * to last st. P1.
3rd row K1. *yo. K1. yo. P7. Rep from * to

YOU'LL NEED
YARN ❸
Bernat® Big Ball Baby Sport
(12.3oz /350g)
1 ball Contrast A 21420 Baby Pink
1 ball Contrast B 21005 Baby White

NEEDLES
Set of four size 4 (3.5mm) double-pointed knitting needles. Size 4 (3.5mm) knitting needles *or size to obtain gauge*

ADDITIONAL
Stuffing.
Black yarn for embroidery

end of row.
4th row *K7. P3. Rep from * to last st. P1.
5th row K1. *yo. K3. yo. P7. Rep from * to end of row.
6th row *K1tbl. K4. P7. Rep from * to end of row.
7th row K1. *yo. K5. yo. P7. Rep from * to end of row.
8th row *K1tbl. K6. P7. Rep from * to end of row.
9th row K1. *yo. K7. yo. P7. Rep from * to end of row.
10th row *K1tbl. K8. P7. Rep from * to end of row.
11th row K1. *yo. K9. yo. P7. Rep from * to end of row.
12th row *K1tbl. K10. P7. Rep from * to end of row.
13th row K1. *yo. K11. yo. P7. Rep from * to end of row.
14th row *K1tbl. K12. P7. Rep from * to end of row.
Cast off. Sew side edges. Sew Skirt around Body.

STRIPED Jacket

SIZES
To fit chest measurement
6 mos 17" [43cm]
12 mos 18" [45.5cm]
18 mos 19" [48cm]
2 yrs 21" [53.5cm]

Finished chest
6 mos 21" [53.5cm]
12 mos 22" [56cm]
18 mos 23½" [59.5cm]
2 yrs 26" [66cm]

GAUGE
22 sts and 30 rows = 4" [10cm] with
larger needles in stockinette st.
Take time to check your gauge.

INSTRUCTIONS
Note The instructions are written for smallest size. If changes are necessary for larger
sizes the instructions will be written thus
( ). When only one number is given, it applies to all sizes. For ease in working, circle
all numbers pertaining to your size.

BACK
With smaller needles and MC, cast on 57
(61-65-71) sts.
1st row (RS) K1. *P1. K1. Rep from * to end
of row.

2nd row P1. *K1. P1. Rep from * to end of
row.
Rep last 2 rows of (K1. P1) ribbing twice
more, inc 1 (0-0-0) st at center of last row.
58 (61-65-71) sts.

Change to larger needles and proceed in Stripe Pat as follows
With A, work 4 rows in stockinette st.
With MC, knit 2 rows (garter st).
These 6 rows form Stripe Pat.
Cont in Stripe Pat until work from beg
measures 6 (7-7½-8)" [15 (18-19-20.5)cm],
ending with a WS row.

Shape armholes Cast off 5 (6-6-6) sts beg
next 2 rows. 48 (49-53-59) sts.
Cont even in pat until armholes measure

5½ (5½-5½-6)" [14 (14-14-15)cm], ending
with a WS row.

Shape shoulders Cast off 11 (11-13-16) sts
beg next 2 rows. Leave rem 26 (27-27-27)
sts on a st holder.

LEFT FRONT
**With smaller needles and MC, cast on 29
(31-33-35) sts.
Work 6 rows in (K1. P1) ribbing as given for
Back.
Change to larger needles and proceed in
Stripe Pat as given for Back until work from
beg measures 6 (7-7½-8)" [15 (18-19-20.5)
cm],** ending with a WS row.

Shape armhole: Next row (RS) Cast off 5 (6-5-6) sts. Knit to end of row. 24 (25-27-29) sts. Cont even in pat until armhole measures 3" [7.5cm], ending with a purl row.

Shape neck: Next row (RS) K17 (17-19-22). Turn. Leave rem sts on a st holder. Purl 1 row. Dec 1 st at neck edge on next 3 rows, then on every following alt row 3 times more. 11 (11-13-16) sts.

Cont even in pat until armhole measures same length as Back to shoulder, ending with a WS row. Cast off.

RIGHT FRONT

Work from ** to ** as given for Left Front, ending with a RS row.

Shape armhole: Next row (WS) Cast off 5 (6-5-6) sts. Purl to end of row. 24 (25-27-29) sts.

Cont even in pat until armhole measures 3" [7.5cm], ending with a RS row.

Shape neck: Next row (WS) P17 (17-19-22). Turn. Leave rem sts on a st holder. Dec 1 st at neck edge on next 3 rows, then on every following alt row 3 times more. 11 (11-13-16) sts.

Cont even in pat until armhole measures same length as Back to shoulder, ending with a RS row. Cast off.

SLEEVES

With smaller needles and MC, cast on 31 (33-33-35) sts. Work 6 rows in (K1. P1) ribbing as given for Back.

Change to larger needles and beg with A, proceed in Stripe Pat as given for Back, inc 1 st each end of needle on next and every following alt row to 53 (43-39-41) sts, then every following 4th row to 61 (61-61-67) sts.

Cont even in pat until work from beg measures 6 (7½-8-9)" [15 (19-20.5-23)cm], ending with a WS row. Place marker at each end of last row. Work a further 8 rows in pat. Cast off.

FINISHING

Pin garment pieces to measurements. Cover with a damp cloth, leaving cloth to dry.

Neckband Sew shoulder seams. With RS of work facing, smaller needles and MC, K7 (8-8-7) from right front st holder. Pick up and knit 18 (19-19-22) sts up right front neck to shoulder. K26 (27-27-27) from back st holder, dec 3 (2-2-2) sts evenly across. Pick up and knit 18 (19-19-22) sts down left front neck edge. K7 (8-8-7) from left front st holder. 73 (79-79-83) sts.
1st row (WS) P2. *K1. P1. Rep from * to last st. P1.
2nd row K2. *P1. K1. Rep from * to last st. K1. Rep last 2 rows twice more. Cast off in ribbing.

Buttonhole band With RS of work facing, smaller needles and MC, pick up and knit 53 (59-62-65) sts down left front edge to top of neckband.
1st row (WS) P1. *K1. P1. Rep from * to end of row.
2nd row (Buttonhole row) Rib 3 sts. *yo. K2tog. Rib 13 (15-16-17) sts. Rep from * to last 5 sts. yo. K2tog. Rib 3 sts.
Work 3 rows more in (K1. P1) ribbing. Cast off in ribbing.

Button band With RS of work facing, smaller needles and MC, pick up and knit 53 (59-62-65) sts up right front edge to top of neckband.
Work as given for buttonhole band, omitting references to buttonholes.
Sew in sleeves, placing rows above markers along cast off sts of Fronts and Back to form square armholes. Sew side and sleeve seams, matching stripes.

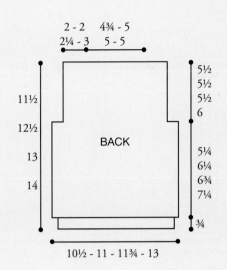

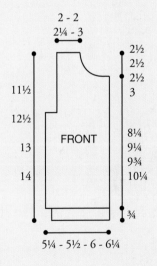

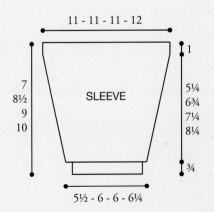

TURTLE Hat and Scarf

YOU'LL NEED

YARN
Bernat® Softee Baby
(Ombres: 4.25oz /120g;
Solids: 5oz/140g)
All Sizes 1 ball each

HAT
Main Color (MC) (31307 Rock-A-Bye
Baby)
Contrast A (02002 Pale Blue)

SCARF
Main Color (MC) (31307 Rock-A-Bye
Baby)
Contrast A (02002 Pale Blue)
Contrast B (30208 Bongo Blue)

NEEDLES
Sizes 5 (3.75mm) and 6 (4mm) knitting
needles *or size to obtain gauge*

SIZES
Hat
To fit child's head
6 mos (12 mos-18 mos-2 yrs)
Scarf
Approx 5 x 40" [12.5 x 101.5cm].

GAUGE
22 sts and 30 rows = 4" [10cm] with larger
needles in stockinette st.
Take time to check your gauge.

INSTRUCTIONS
Note The instructions are written for smallest size. If changes are necessary for larger
sizes the instructions will be written thus
( ). When only one number is given, it applies to all sizes. For ease in working, circle
all numbers pertaining to your size.

HAT
With MC and smaller needles, cast on 79
(88-94-100) sts.
Knit 5 rows (garter st), noting first row is WS.

Change to larger needles and proceed as follows:
With A, work 6 rows in stockinette st, ending with a purl row.
Next 2 rows With MC, knit 2 rows (garter st).
Rep last 8 rows of Stripe Pat 2 (2-3-3) times more, dec 0 (3-3-3) sts evenly across last row. 79 (85-91-97) sts.

Shape top Keeping cont of pat, proceed as follows
1st row (RS) *K11 (12-13-14). K2tog. Rep from * to last st. K1. 73 (79-85-91) sts.
Work 3 rows even in pat.
Next row *K10 (11-12-13). K2tog. Rep from * to last st. K1. 67 (73-79-85) sts.
Work 3 rows even in pat.
Next row *K9 (10-11-12). K2tog. Rep from * to last st. K1. 61 (67-73-79) sts.
Next row P1. *P2tog. P8 (9-10-11). Rep from * to end of row. 55 (61-67-73) sts.
Next row *K7 (8-9-10). K2tog. Rep from * to last st. K1. 49 (55-61-67) sts.
Next row P1. *P2tog. P6 (7-8-9). Rep from * to end of row. 43 (49-55-61) sts.
Next row *K5 (6-7-8). K2tog. Rep from * to last st. K1. 37 (43-49-55) sts.
Next row P1. *P2tog. P4 (5-6-7). Rep from * to end of row. 31 (37-43-49) sts.
Keeping cont of pat, work 10 rows even in Stripe Pat.
Next row *K3 (4-5-6). K2tog. Rep from * to last st. K1. 25 (31-37-43) sts.
Next row P1. *P2tog. P2 (3-4-5). Rep from * to end of row. 19 (25-31-37) sts.
Next row *K1 (2-3-4). K2tog. Rep from * to last st. K1. 13 (19-25-31) sts.

Sizes 18 mos and 2 yrs only: Next row P1. *P2tog. P(2-3). Rep from * to end of row. (19-25) sts.
Next row *K(1-2). K2tog. Rep from * to last st. K1. (13-19) sts.

All sizes With MC, work 13 (13-11-11) rows even in pat.
Next row *K2tog. Rep from * to last st. K1. 7 (9-7-9) sts.
With MC, work 10 rows in stockinette st even.
Next row *K2tog. Rep from * to last st. K1. 4 (5-4-5) sts.

Break MC leaving a long end. Draw end through rem sts and fasten securely. Sew center back seam.

SCARF
Note When working from Chart, wind small balls of the colors to be used, one for each separate area of color in the design. Start new colors at appropriate points. To change colors, twist the two yarns around each other where they meet on WS to avoid a hole.
With A and smaller needles, cast on 26 sts. Knit 3 rows (garter st), noting 1st row is WS and inc 2 sts evenly across last row. 28 sts.
Change to larger needles and proceed as follows
**1st row (RS) Knit.
2nd row K3. Purl to last 3 sts. K3.***
Rep last 2 rows twice more.

Proceed as follows
Next row (RS) With A, K5. Work 1st row of Chart, reading row from right to left. With A, K5.
Next row With A, K3. P2. Work 2nd row of Chart, reading row from left to right. With A, P2. K3.
Chart is now in position. Work in Chart to end of chart.

Rep from ** to *** 3 times more.**

Proceed in Stripe Pat as follows
With A, knit 2 rows.
With MC, work 8 rows in stockinette st, keeping 2 sts at each side of Scarf in garter st.
Last 10 rows form Stripe Pat.
Cont in Stripe Pat until work from beg measures approx 36" [91.5cm], ending with 2 rows of A.
Work from ** to ** as given above, dec 2 sts evenly across last row. 26 sts. n
Change to smaller needles and knit 3 rows. Cast off knitwise (WS).

Chart

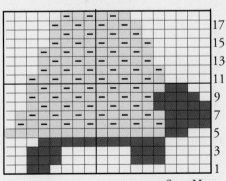

Start Here

☐ = With MC, knit on RS and purl on WS.

⊟ = With MC, purl on RS and knit on WS.

☐ = With A, knit on RS and purl on WS.

■ = With B, knit on RS and purl on WS.

TURTLE Pullover

YOU'LL NEED

YARN ③
Bernat® Softee Baby
(Solids: 5oz/140g)
All Sizes Main Color (MC) 1 ball
(02002 Pale Blue)
Contrast A 1 ball (30208 Bongo
Blue)
Bernat® Softee Baby
(Ombres: 4.25oz/120g)
All Sizes Contrast B 1 ball (31307
Rock-A-Bye Baby)

NEEDLES
Sizes 4 (3.5mm) and 6 (4mm)
knitting needles *or size to obtain
gauge*

ADDITIONAL
2 st holders

SIZES

To fit chest measurement
6 mos 17" [43cm]
12 mos 18" [45.5cm]
18 mos 19" [48cm]
2 yrs 21" [53.5cm]

Finished chest
6 mos 21" [53.5cm]
12 mos 22½" [57cm]
18 mos 24" [61cm]
2 yrs 26" [66cm]

GAUGE
22 sts and 30 rows = 4" [10cm] with larger
needles in St st.
Take time to check your gauge.

INSTRUCTIONS
Note The instructions are written for
smallest size. If changes are necessary for
larger sizes the instructions will be written
thus ( ). When only one number is given,
it applies to all sizes. For ease in working,
circle all numbers pertaining to your size.

FRONT
Note When working from Chart II, wind

small balls of the colors to be used, one for
each separate area of color in the design.
Start new colors at appropriate points. To
change colors, twist the two yarns around
each other where they meet on WS to
avoid a hole.

**With smaller needles and B, cast on 57
(61-65-71) sts. Break B.
1st row (RS) With MC, K1. *P1. K1. Rep from
* to end of row.
2nd row P1. *K1. P1. Rep from * to end of
row.
Rep last 2 rows of (K1. P1) ribbing twice
more, inc 1 st at center of last row. 58 (62-
66-72) sts.

Change to larger needles and proceed in
Stripe Pat as follows:

With B, knit 2 rows (garter st).
With MC, work 6 rows in stockinette st.
These 8 rows form Stripe Pat.**
Rep last 8 rows of Stripe Pat 0 (0-1-2)
time(s) more, then first 4 (6-6-4) rows once

Place chart as follows
Note Chart is shown on page 31
Next row (RS) With MC, K14 (16-18-21).
Work 1st row of Chart, reading row from
right to left. With MC, K14 (16-18-21).
Next row With MC, P14 (16-18-21). Work
2nd row of Chart, reading row from left to
right. With MC, P14 (16-18-21).
Chart is now in position.
Cont in Chart until work from beg mea-
sures 6 (7-7½-8)" [15 (18-19-20.5cm], end-
ing with a WS row.
Shape armholes Keeping cont of Chart,

cast off 5 (6-6-6) sts beg next 2 rows. 48 (50-54- 60) sts.

Cont even in Chart to end of chart. With MC, cont even in stockinette st until armholes measure 3" [7.5cm], ending with a purl row.

Shape neck: Next row (RS) K17 (17-19-22). Turn. Leave rem sts on a spare needle. Dec 1 st at neck edge on next 4 rows, then on every following alt row twice. 11 (11-13-16) sts.

Cont even in stockinette st until armhole measures 5½ (5½-5½-6)" [14 (14-14-15) cm], ending with a purl row. Cast off.

With RS of work facing, slip next 14 (16-16-16) sts on a st holder. Join MC to rem sts and knit to end of row.
Dec 1 st at neck edge on next 4 rows, then on every following alt row twice more. 11 (11-13-16) sts.
Cont even in stockinette st until armhole measures 5½ (5½-5½-6)" [14 (14-14-15) cm], ending with a purl row. Cast off.

BACK
Work from ** to ** as given for Front. Cont in Stripe Pat until work from beg measures 6 (7-7½-8)" [15 (18-19-20.5)cm], ending with a WS row.

Shape armholes Cast off 5 (6-6-6) sts beg next 2 rows. 48 (50-54- 60) sts.
Cont even in Stripe Pat until armholes measure 5½ (5½-5½-6)" [14 (14-14-15)cm], ending with a WS row.

Shape shoulders Cast off 11 (11-13-16) sts beg next 2 rows. Leave rem 26 (28-28-28) sts on a st holder.

SLEEVES
With smaller needles and B, cast on 31 (33-33-35) sts. Break B.
With MC, work 6 rows in (K1. P1) ribbing as given for Front.
Change to larger needles and proceed in Stripe Pat as given for Front, inc 1 st each end of needle on next and every following alt row to 55 (43-39-41) sts,

then every following 4th row to 61 (61-61-67) sts.

Cont even in Stripe Pat until work from beg measures 6 (7½-8-9)" [15 (19-20.5-23) cm], ending with a WS row. Place a marker at each end of last row. Work a further 8 rows in Stripe Pat. Cast off.

FINISHING
Pin garment pieces to measurements. Cover with a damp cloth, leaving cloth to dry.

Neckband Sew right shoulder seam. With RS of work facing, smaller needles and MC, pick up and knit 18 (19-19-22) sts down left front neck edge. K14 (16-16-16) from front st holder. Pick up and knit 18 (19-19-22) sts up right front neck to shoulder. K26 (28-28-28) from back st holder, dec 3 sts evenly across. 73 (79-79-85) sts.
1st row (WS) P1. *K1. P1. Rep from * to end of row.
2nd row K1. *P1. K1.
Rep from * to end of row.
Rep last 2 rows of (K1. P1) ribbing twice more.
With B, work 1 row in (K1. P1) ribbing. Cast off in ribbing.
Sew left shoulder seam and neck band.
Sew in sleeves, placing rows above markers along cast off sts of Fronts and Back to form square armholes. Sew side and sleeve seams, matching stripes.

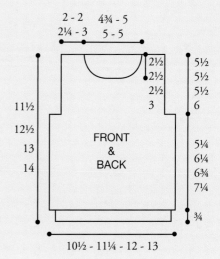

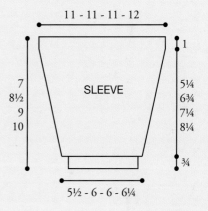

Chart

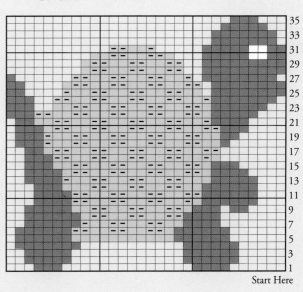

Start Here

Key

 = With MC, knit on RS and purl on WS.

☐ = With B, knit on RS and purl on WS.

⊟ = With B, purl on RS and knit on WS

▓ = With A, knit on RS and purl on WS.

TURTLE Toy

MEASUREMENT
Approx 13" [33cm] in diameter.

GAUGE
16 sts and 19 rows = 4" [10cm] in St st with
2 strands tog.
Take time to check your gauge.

TURTLE
Shell
With 2 strands of MC, cast on 7 sts.
1st row (WS) (Inc 1 st in next st)
6 times. K1. 13 sts.
2nd, 4th and 6th rows Purl.
3rd row (Inc 1 st in next st) 12 times. K1. 25
sts.
5th row (Inc 1 st in next st) 25 times. 50 sts.
**7th row K1. *P3tog. (K1. P1. K1) all in next
st. Rep from * to last st. K1.
8th row Purl.
9th row K1. *(K1. P1. K1) all in next st. P3tog.
Rep from * to last st. K1.

10th row Purl.
Rep 7th to 10th rows for Trinity St Pat.
11th row As 7th row.
12th and 14th rows Purl.
13th row As 9th row.
15th row K1. *M1. P3tog. (K1. P1. K1) all in
next st. Rep from * to last st. K1.
16th row P4. *M1P. P5. Rep from * to last 3
sts. M1P. P3.
17th row K1. *(K1. P1. K1) all in next st. K1.
(K1. P1. K1) all in next st. P3tog. Rep from *
to last st. K1.
Next row Purl.** 98 sts.
Rep from ** to ** once more, placing sts on
a circular needle when necessary. 196 sts.
Work 8 rows even in Trinity St Pat, ending
with a RS row. Join in rnd. Place marker at
end of last row.
Next rnd K1. *K2tog. K3. Rep from * around.
157 sts.
Knit 12 rnds even. Cast off.

Belly
***With 2 strands of A, cast on 6 sts.
1st row (RS) (Inc 1 st in next st) 5 times. K1.
11 sts.
2nd and alt rows Purl.
3rd row *Inc 1 st in next st. Rep from * to
last st. K1. 21 sts.
5th row *K1. Inc 1 st in next st. Rep from *
to last st. K1. 31 sts.***
7th row *K2. Inc 1 st in next st. Rep from *
to last st. K1. 41 sts.
9th row *K3. Inc 1 st in next st. Rep from *
to last st. K1. 51 sts.
Cont in same manner, inc 10 sts as before
on every following alt row to 201 sts, placing sts on circular needle when necessary.
Cast off. Sew seam.
Sew Belly to Shell along marked row, leaving opening for stuffing. Stuff body. Sew
opening closed.

Head and Neck
Work from *** to *** as given for Belly.
Beg with a purl row, work 12 rows in St st.

Next row (WS) P1. (P3tog) 10 times. 11 sts.
Beg with a knit row, work 16 rows in stockinette st. Cast off.
Sew back seam. Stuff head, leaving neck
unstuffed.
Fold cast off edge in half and sew to
marked row of Shell. Attach Head to Shell
as shown in picture.

Legs (make 4)
With 2 strands of A, cast on 6 sts.
1st row (RS) (Inc 1 st in next st)
5 times. K1. 11 sts.
2nd row Purl.
3rd row *Inc 1 st in next st. Rep from * to
last st. K1. 21 sts.
Beg with a purl row, work 5 rows in stockinette st.
Next row (RS) *K1. K2tog. Rep from * to
end of row. 14 sts.
Beg with a purl row, work 7 rows in stockinette st. Cast off.
Sew back seam. Stuff legs to half of length.
Fold cast off edge in half and sew to
marked row of Shell as shown in picture.

Tail
With 2 strands of A, cast on 3 sts.
Proceed in stockinette st, inc 1 st each end
of needle on 3rd and every following alt
row to 21 sts, ending with a purl row. Cast
off. Sew center seam.
Fold cast off edge in half and sew to
marked row of Shell as shown in picture.
With brown yarn, embroider eyes and
mouth as shown in picture.

TURTLE Blanket

YOU'LL NEED

YARN ③
1 ball each
Bernat® Softee Baby
(Solids: 5oz/140g)
Main Color (MC) (30208 Bongo Blue)
Contrast A (02002 Pale Blue)
Contrast B (0200 White)

Bernat® Softee Baby
(Ombres: 4.25oz /120g)
Contrast C (31307 Rock-A-Bye Baby)

NEEDLES
Size 7 (4.5mm) knitting needles. Size
7 (4.5mm) circular needle 24" (60cm)
or size to obtain gauge

MEASUREMENT
Approx 36" [91.5cm] square.

GAUGE
21 sts and 29 rows = 4" [10cm] in St st.
Take time to check your gauge.

INSTRUCTIONS
Note When working from Chart, wind
small balls of the colors to be used, one for
each separate area of color in the design.
Start new colors at appropriate points. To
change colors, twist the two yarns around
each other where they meet on WS to
avoid a hole.

Panel A (make 1)
With MC, cast on 39 sts.
**1st and 2nd rows Knit, noting 1st row is RS.
3rd row K1. *P1. K1. Rep from * to end of row.
4th row K1. *K1. P1. Rep from * to last 2 sts.
K2.
Rep 1st to 4th rows for Pat until work from
beg measures 7" [18cm], ending with a WS
row.**

Proceed as follows
Work Chart to end of chart, reading RS
rows from right to left and WS rows from
left to right, having A as Color 1.
Chart is shown on this page.

With MC, work from ** to ** as given
above.

Proceed as follows
***With A, beg with a knit row, work 4 rows
in stockinette st.
With B, work 2 rows in stockinette st.

With MC, knit 2 rows (garter st).
With B, work 4 rows in stockinette st.
With A, work 2 rows in stockinette st.
With MC, knit 2 rows (garter st).
These 16 rows form Stripe Pat.

Work in Stripe Pat for 7" [18cm], ending
with 2 rows of A or B.***

With MC, work from ** to ** as given
above. Cast off.

Panel B (make 1)
With B, cast on 39 sts.
Work Chart to end of chart, having B as
Color 1.
With MC, work from ** to ** as given for
Panel A.
Work from *** to *** as given for Panel A.
With MC, work from ** to ** as given for
Panel A.
Work Chart to end of chart, having A as
Color 1. Cast off.

Chart

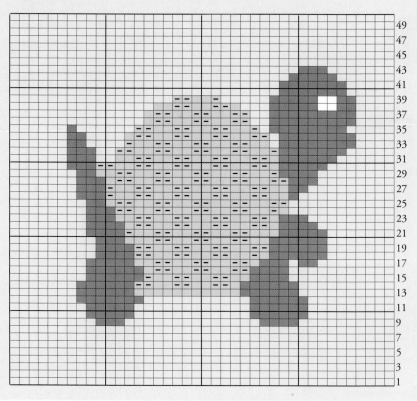

49
47
45
43
41
39
37
35
33
31
29
27
25
23
21
19
17
15
13
11
9
7
5
3
1

☐ = With Color 1, knit
on RS and purl on WS.

☐ = With C, knit on RS
and purl on WS.

▬ = With C, purl on RS
and knit on WS.

▇ = With MC, knit on RS
and purl on WS.

Panel C (make 1)

With MC, cast on 39 sts.
With MC, work from ** to ** as given for Panel A.
Work from *** to *** as given for Panel A.
With MC, work from ** to ** as given for Panel A.
Work Chart to end of chart, having B as Color 1.
With MC, work from ** to ** as given for Panel A. Cast off.

Panel D (make 1)

With A, cast on 39 sts.
Work from *** to *** as given for Panel A.
Work Chart to end of chart, having A as Color 1.
With MC, work from ** to ** as given for

Panel A.
Work from *** to *** as given for Panel A.
Cast off.

Panel E (make 1)

With MC, cast on 39 sts.
With MC, work from ** to ** as given for Panel A.
Work Chart to end of chart, having B as Color 1.
With MC, work from ** to ** as given for Panel A.
Work from *** to *** as given for Panel A.
With MC, work from ** to ** as given for Panel A. Cast off.

FINISHING

Pin panels to measurements. Cover with a

damp cloth, leaving cloth to dry.
Sew panels tog in the following sequence:
A, B, C, D, E.

Top and bottom edging With RS facing, circular needle and C, pick up and knit 180 sts evenly across top of Blanket. Do not join in rnd. Working back and forth across needle, knit 4 rows. Cast off loosely knitwise.
Rep for bottom of Blanket.

Side edging With RS facing, circular needle and MC, pick up and knit 186 sts evenly along side of Blanket. Knit 4 rows. Cast off loosely knitwise.
Rep for other side.

YOU'LL NEED

YARN (3)
Bernat® Big Ball Baby Sport
(12.3oz/350g)
1 ball Main Color (MC)
(21005 Baby White)
1 ball Contrast A (21730 Popsicle
Blue)

NEEDLES
Size 6 (4mm) knitting needles *or size
to obtain gauge*

ADDITIONAL
Stuffing
Small length of black embroidery floss
Pair of size 4 mm (U.S. 6) double-
pointed needles for I-cord

MEASUREMENT
Toy Approx 8½" [21.5cm] tall x 5" [12.5cm]
wide.

GAUGE
22 sts and 30 rows = 4" [10cm] in stockinette stitch.
Take time to check your gauge.

INSTRUCTIONS
Front and Back (make 2 pieces alike)
With MC, cast on 8 sts.
1st row (RS) Knit.
2nd row Purl.
3rd row Cast on 4 sts. Knit to end of row.
12 sts.
4th row P2tog. Purl to end of row.
5th row Cast on 4 sts. Knit to last 2 sts.
K2tog.
6th row As 4th row.
7th row Cast on 3 sts. Knit to last 2 sts.
K2tog.
8th and 9th rows Rep 6th and 7th rows. 16 sts.
10th row Purl to last st. Inc1P in last st.
11th row Inc in first st. Knit to last 2 sts.
K2tog.
12th and 13th rows Rep 10th and 11th

rows. 18 sts.
14th row As 10th row.
15th row Inc 1 st in first st. Knit to end of
row.
16th and alt rows Purl.
17th row As 11th row.
19th, 21st, 23rd and 25th rows As 15th row.
24 sts at end of 25th row.
26th row Purl.
Cont even in stockinette st until work from
beg measures 6" [15cm], ending with a
purl row.

Proceed as follows
1st row K2tog. Knit to end of row.
2nd row Purl.
3rd to 6th rows Rep 1st and 2nd rows
twice more. 21 sts.
7th row K2tog. Knit to last st. Inc 1 st in last st.
8th row Purl.
9th row K2tog. Knit to end of row.
10th row Purl.
11th row K2tog. Knit to last st. Inc 1 st in
last st.
12th row Purl to last 2 sts. P2tog.
13th and 14th rows Rep 11th and 12th
rows. 18 sts.
15th row As 11th row.
16th row Inc1P. Purl to last 2 sts. P2tog.
17th row Cast off 3 sts. Knit to last st.
Inc 1 st in last st.
18th row Inc1P. Purl to end of row.
19th and 20th row Rep 17th and 18th rows.
16 sts.
21st row Cast off 4 sts. Knit to end of row.
22nd row Purl.
23rd and 24th rows Rep 21st and 22nd
rows.
Cast off rem 8 sts.

Legs (make 2)
With A, cast on 9 sts.
Work 4 rows stockinette st.
With MC, work 2 rows stockinette st.
With A, work 4 rows stockinette st.

Rep last 6 rows twice more.
With MC, work 2 rows stockinette st. Break MC
With A, work 2 rows stockinette st.

Shape foot: 1st row (RS) K4. M1. K1. M1. K4.
2nd and alt rows Purl.
3rd row K5. M1. K1. M1. K5.
5th row K6. M1. K1. M1. K6.
7th row K7. M1. K1. M1. K7. 17 sts.
8th row Purl.
Dec 1 st each end of next and following alt
row once more. 13 sts.
Next row (WS) P1. (P2tog. P1) 4 times. 9 sts.
Cast off. Stuff Legs lightly.

Arms (make 2)
With A and pair of double-pointed needles,
cast on 5 sts.

1st row K5. Slide sts to opposite end of
needle.
Rep last row for I-cord, working in Stripe
Pat as follows: 2 rows A; 2 rows MC.
Cont in Stripe Pat until Arm measures
3" [7.5cm]. Break yarn. Draw yarn tightly
through rem sts and fasten securely.

FINISHING
Place Front and Back pieces tog with WS
facing each other. Sew outer edges tog
leaving an opening along straight edge to
insert stuffing. Stuff lightly. Sew opening
closed. Sew Legs and Arms in position as
shown in picture. With A, embroider eyes,
using satin stitch. With black embroidery
floss, embroider mouth and eyebrows using outline stitch.

MONSTER-IN-STRIPES

YOU'LL NEED

YARN ③
Bernat® Big Ball Baby Sport
(Solids: 12.3oz/350g)
1 ball Contrast A 21700 Tangerine
1 ball Contrast B 21402 Strawberry

Bernat® Big Ball Baby Sport
(Ombres: 9.8z/280g)
1 ball Contrast C 24702 Punch Fun

NEEDLES
Set of four size 4 (3.5mm) double-pointed knitting needles. Size 4 (3.5mm) circular knitting needle 16" [40cm] long *or size to obtain gauge*

ADDITIONAL
Stuffing.
Small amount of green yarn for embroidery.
White piece of felt for eyes.

MEASUREMENT
Approx 10½" [26.5cm] tall, excluding legs.

GAUGE
25 sts and 31 rows = 4" [10cm] in St st.
Take time to check your gauge.

INSTRUCTIONS
Monster Body
Stripe Pat
With A, knit 6 rnds.
With B, knit 6 rnds.
With A, knit 2 rnds.
With B, knit 2 rnds.
These 16 rnds form Stripe Pat.

With double-pointed needles and A, cast on 6 sts. Divide sts onto 3 needles (2 sts on each needle). Join in rnd, placing a marker on first st.
Proceed in Stripe Pat as follows
**1st rnd (Inc 1 st in next st) 6 times. 12 sts.
2nd and alt rnds Knit.

3rd rnd (Inc 1 st in next st. K1) 6 times. 18 sts.
5th rnd (Inc 1 st in next st. K2) 6 times. 24 sts.
7th rnd With B, (Inc 1 st in next st. K3) 6 times. 30 sts.
9th rnd (Inc 1 st in next st. K4) 6 times. 36 sts.**
11th rnd (Inc 1 st in next st. K5) 6 times. 42 sts.
12th rnd With B, as 2nd rnd.
First 12 rnds of Stripe Pat are completed. Cont in same manner, keeping cont of Stripe Pat, inc 6 sts on next and every following alt rnd until there are 114 sts. (Change to circular needle to accommodate all sts when necessary). Place marker at end of last rnd.
Cont even in Stripe Pat until work from marked rnd measures 3" [7.5cm].
Next rnd (K17. K2tog) 6 times. 108 sts.
Work 3 rnds even in pat.
Next rnd (K16. K2tog) 6 times. 102 sts.
Work 3 rnds even in pat.
Next rnd (K15. K2tog) 6 times. 96 sts.
Work 3 rnds even in pat.
Next rnd (K14. K2tog) 6 times. 90 sts.
Work 3 rnds even in pat.
Next rnd (K13. K2tog) 6 times. 84 sts.
Work 3 rnds even in pat.
Next rnd (K12. K2tog) 6 times. 78 sts. Place marker at end of rnd.
With A only, cont even until work from last marked rnd measures approx 3" [7.5cm].

Shape top: 1st rnd With B, (K11. K2tog) 6 times. 72 sts.
2nd and alt rnds Purl.
3rd rnd (K10. K2tog) 6 times. 66 sts.
5th rnd (K9. K2tog) 6 times. 60 sts.
6th rnd Purl. Break B.
7th rnd With A, (K8. K2tog) 6 times. 54 sts.
9th rnd (K7. K2tog) 6 times. 48 sts.
Stuff Body.
11th rnd (K6. K2tog) 6 times. 42 sts.
13th rnd (K5. K2tog) 6 times. 36 sts.
15th rnd (K4. K2tog) 6 times. 30 sts.
17th rnd (K3. K2tog) 6 times. 24 sts.
19th rnd (K2tog) 12 times. 12 sts. Break yarn, leaving a long end. Draw end tightly through rem sts and fasten securely.

Left Leg
Foot With A only, work from ** to ** as given for Body.
Knit 6 rnds.
1st rnd (K2tog. K4) 6 times. 30 sts.
2nd and alt rnds Knit.
3rd rnd (K2tog. K3) 6 times. 24 sts.
5th rnd (K2tog. K2) 6 times. 18 sts.
7th rnd (K2tog. K1) 6 times. 12 sts.
Break A.
Stuff Foot.
With C, knit in rnds for 4" [10cm]. Cast off. Do not stuff C section.

Right Leg
Work as given for Left Leg, substituting B for A.
Sew Legs in position.

Ears (make 2)
With B, cast on 3 sts.
1st row (RS) (Inc 1 st in next st) twice. K1. 5 sts.
2nd and alt rows Purl.
3rd row (Inc 1 st in next st) 4 times. K1. 9 sts.
5th row (Inc 1 st in next st) 8 times. K1. 17 sts.
7th row Inc 1 st in first st. Knit to last 2 sts. Inc 1 st in next st. K1. 19 sts.
8th row Purl.
Knit 2 rows.
Beg with a purl row, work 3 rows in reverse stockinette st, inc 1 st each end of needle on next and following alt row. 23 sts. Cast off knitwise (WS).
Sew Ears in position.

Hair
Cut C 5" [12.5cm] long. Taking 10 strands tog knot into hair at top of "Head". Trim fringe evenly.
With white felt cut out eyes and using green yarn, sew in position.

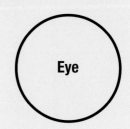

Eye

ZIG-ZAG Blanket

YOU'LL NEED

YARN

Bernat® Big Ball Baby Sport
(Solids: 12.3oz/350g)
Contrast A 1 ball (21700 Tangerine)
Contrast B 1 ball (21402 Strawberry)

Bernat® Big Ball Baby Sport
(Ombres: 9.8oz/280g)
Contrast C 1 ball (24702 Punch Fun)

NEEDLE

Size 6 (4mm) circular knitting needle
36" [90cm] long *or size to obtain
gauge*

MEASUREMENT

Approx 29 x 36" [73.5 x 91.5cm].

GAUGE

22 sts and 30 rows = 4" [10cm] in stockinette st. *Take time to check your gauge.*

INSTRUCTIONS

With C, cast on 193 sts. Do not join in rnd.
Working back and forth across needle, knit
3 rows, noting 1st row is WS and inc 10 sts
evenly across last row. 203 sts.

Proceed in Zig-Zag pat as follows
1st row (RS) With A, K5. K2tog. *K4. (K1. yo.
K1) all in next st. K4. Sl1. K2tog. psso. Rep
from * to last 16 sts. K4. (K1. yo. K1) all in
next st. K4. Ssk. K5.
2nd row K4. Purl to last 4 sts. K4.
3rd and 4th rows As 1st and 2nd rows.
5th row As 1st row.
6th row Knit.
7th to 9th rows With C, rep 1st to 3rd rows.
10th row Knit.
11th to 16th rows With B, as 1st to 6th rows.
17th to 20th rows As 7th to 10th rows.
These 20 rows form pat.
Cont in pat until work from beg measures
approx 35" [89cm], ending with 6 rows of
A or B.
Next row With C, knit, dec 10 sts evenly
across. 193 sts.
Knit 2 rows. Cast off knitwise (WS).